I have made liberal use of the word God
throughout this book.
I might well have said existence, source,
divinity, the ground of being,
unity or any number of other terms.
Readers are invited to not get stuck on a word.

Yoni verse
BURLESQUE

The Poetry of Aisha Wolfe

Emerging Now Press

ISBN: 978-0-9576339-0-2

First published in the United Kingdom June 2013
by Emerging Now Press.

www.emergingnow.co.uk

Emerging Now Press

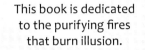

This book is dedicated
to the purifying fires
that burn illusion.

It is for all those who seek deeper
than surface level splashes.
Truth is a sharp sword sheathed,
but sometimes it needs
to be taken out and polished.

It is a gift of love and prayer for peace.

You are a point of light
between two eternal darknesses.
Make it matter.

Part One

Maps to the Underworld

DEAR WOMAN

Woman,
You belong to the night.
You have blood on your thighs
and furze in your hair.
You smell of loamy fertile soil.
Your breasts give life.
Your sex is a mystery school
leading to the holy of holies.

Turn your eyes inward.
Use owls' vision to see where you come from.
Slip beneath the surface,
Feel yourself become full.

Make a marriage to the moon.

Divorce the false gods of intellect and reason.
Find meaning in your dreams.
And in the secrets of your body.

Follow no authority -
But your own true nature.

Make a sacred fire.
And throw on it all that you would use to harm yourself.
Make kindling from shame.

Let your dance be wild.
Your voice be honest.
And your heart untamed.

Be cyclical.
Don't make sense.

Initiate yourself.
Initiate yourself.

THE DESCENT

At the first gate,
she became initiate.

At the second she was given
a dark round bowl,
filled with water.

At the third gate,
she played with fire.

At the fourth,
she gave it away.

At the fifth gate,
she learned the language of the moon.

At the sixth,
she saw through veils.

At the seventh,
she was kissed by a cobra.

She died.
She was reborn.

She has
The blue lotus flowers.

THE INVITATION

For a very long time.
I heard God whispering to me.
"I keep calling to you, why do you not come?"

And now I know the answer.

I could not come.

Until I knew
there was nowhere else to go.

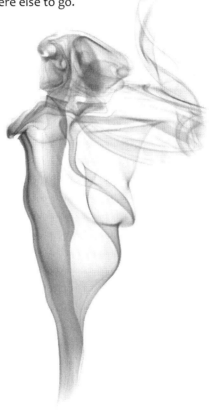

FAMILY TREE

Isabella Morrison was my mother's mother.
My grand-mother.
Responsible for a part of me, which wasn't my body.

She was tender with me,
But like granite with my mother.
She was small.
Like a bird.
Born under a Cancer sun.
She lived til 81,
and died from what doctors called,
a "system shutdown".

I don't recognise her in photos
as a young woman.
I knew her as my Nana.
She liked to dance.
But not to be touched.

When I was little, I heard she had
"never been bothered by her husband much."
Had one daughter, one son.

She loved honey and was fiercely bitter.
She raised me as much as my mother.
Like a tug of war.
Lived in Leith all her life,
and always had clean windows.

Her mother had died giving birth to her sister.
At the end of her life she told me,
she had never known love.

She did not slip peacefully into death.
She wanted to be held.
She cried out to Mary.
She cried out to Mother.
She was selectively Christian.
Kept a bible, but did not read it.
Believed in God.
But not that he would receive her.

When she died my mother was free.
But would not allow it.

She lives on in my heart and my bones.
And whenever I dance and touch.
When I love.
Whenever I take care of me.
I know I set my Nana free.

She lives on in my soul.
With a sharp tongue and a wisdom.
She fought with all her days.

The struggles of her life,
have not been in vain.

When I was young
there was so much fear.
But she gave me pomegranates.
And the seeds found root.
When it was very dark.
I would dream of wolves
breaking in through those clean windows.

And when I died.
They set me free.

To my ancestors.
Be peaceful as you rest in me.
The meaning of your lives
is still unfolding.
Rest and be free in me.
The blossom of our lives
Is still unfurling.

Be still.
I am standing on your shoulders.
Rest.

ALONENESS

Our true friends.
Who want us to be all that we can be,
Will never rescue us from aloneness.

Sometimes, the only place intimacy can be found,
Is in the arms of the darkness of our solitude.

In this place, the soul deepens.
In this place we can become still enough
to witness the hidden pearl
as it forms.

Making love with the darkness,
takes a certain kind of courage.
You will meet some shadows.
And they may seem real and threatening.
But they are teachers, one and all.

In the darkness
you will come to know your own light.
So you need not fear it anymore.
The light of others is always changeable,
and prone to flickering.

When you welcome home your emptiness,
it is a mansion to the infinite.
Which, the banks will not foreclose.

So take a deep breath.
Look all around you at the fading colours.
And simply drop in.

You can quote me on this;
"There is a pearl diver out there somewhere.
Just waiting for you to be ready."

THE BODHISATTVA VOW

Lie down and rest.
You are home and safe.
No more fighting for survival.

Breathe out, it's ok.
Breathe in.
I love you.

I have found a small safe haven,
A mound on the earth, with moss and furs,
with a finely woven shawl of compassion.
I invite the small bewildered orphan,
residing in us all to enter.
Come in through the opening
in the darkest corner of your heart.

An awakened life is your birthright.
As the wonder that you are.
Do you not know that we are all thinking
and feeling and creating this world
at the same time.

The mind, as it is, may present
many persuading reasons to be skeptical.
It is still following the previous suggestions.

"I think, therefore I am, just like everyone else,
therefore I am safe."

So conditioned to measuring the heart's flow.
So little trust in being it.

We can help each other to fully flower.
This is the Garden.

There are no motherless children here.
No being far away from home.

We can expand our capacity to feel it all,
like a new muscle being toned.
Until every single cell in our being
chooses love through fear.

We try to pour the ocean of our soul into a thimble.
Because we are afraid to feel so much.

BELOVED STRUGGLE

You struggle because there is a pay off.
You struggle with struggle because
when you're not in struggle, what is there?

When you don't know what is there.
Then you don't know who you are.
When you don't know who you are.
You won't know how to live.

There is a way to live in the state of unknown.
It is to flow.

You don't need to know.
To flow.
You don't need to learn to let go.
To flow.

Letting go is a natural happening,
When you stop avoiding,
Whatever it is you fear the most.

What you fear the most is waiting for you
In the direction you most resist going.

Down.

If you are miserable,
How miserable can you be?

If you are stuck,
How entangled can you get?

If you are alone,
How far down the secret ladder can you go?

Find out what you are miserable about.
And marry it.

Make love with it.
Day in, day out.

Until you no longer fear its tone.
Until you can no longer look into its face.

And not see Grace.

BLUEPRINT

Look outside.
Look within.
Feel outside.
Feel within.

Repeat this meditation.
Over and over and over again.
Where does outside end
and inside begin?

You think you're a woman.
But you're a palm-full of water.
Reflecting what's projecting.
The moon's daughter.

With nothing to hold you
in a constant shape.

You're re-born in the belly
of the oldest snake.

IN-SPIRAL

Right now.
If you feel you are
moving one step forwards,
and two steps back.
You're SO on track.
The soul's life is not linear.
It moves in-spiral.
If it feels like you are
in the exact same place
you always are.
Stuck.
Send that thought to kingdom come.
You are deeper.
The altitude may be steeper.
But by god.
You can still breathe.

PARADOXYMORON

A problem you will never solve,
is how to separate the darkness from the light.

You will never find good without evil.
You will never see day without night.
You will never untangle wrong from right.

There is no sun without the moon.

All the manifest conflicts in this world
arise from this confusion.

There is as much delusion,
in the light as in the darkness.
But the delusions of light seem more friendly.

You will never solve the problem of your life.
If you believe there is one.

And trying to solve the problems of this dimension,
is like tying yourself to a slutty lie and wondering why
you are so fucking exhausted.

So do I have your attention?

Everyone knows not to look directly at the Sun.

But who knew you'd have to burn
your whole damned town down.

To see the fullness of the Moon.

SEEKING

Looking outside of yourself for the light,
is like chasing the horizon.

And when you hear this,
and refuse to listen,

It is like me telling you.
You will never reach the horizon.
And you responding to me.

"Yes I will."
As you run off desperately seeking,
What was inside you all along.

CAILLEACH

Winter
Dark mother
Raven lover

Thank you for coming to greet me again.

Your daughter who has grown strong enough
to be unafraid of your latitude.
Rooted enough to bend with you.
Finally wrapped inside love's most protective cover.
I have nothing but gratitude.
You taught me the dark was a safe haven.
Howled at me until I buried myself
inside your frozen skirts
deep enough to heal the hurts and find renewal.

Dark
Wind
Snow
Cold
Crone

No man's land

Winter.
I feel you lashing your white tail.
You are not pernicious.
It's just how you are.

From your withered branch.
Blossom.

Flesh from your bone.

It's okay mother, take my hand.
I live now.

HEALING

You can heal and change your life.
You can heal and not.
You can heal and change your ways.
You can heal and not.
You can heal and make amends.
You can heal and be estranged.
You can heal and have friends.
You can heal and be alone.
You can heal and not recover.
Why would you want to re-cover?

You can heal and transform.
You can heal and still die.

You can heal and feel right.
You can heal and feel wrong.

Until you change the word heal
for belong.

THE DARK TIDE

I no longer fear the sly dark tide
when it comes.

On the days when the sun shines
but it feels like it's raining stones.

I have learned to swim into it.

In the out-breath of the Great Mother.

Oracular Bones.

I will read them.

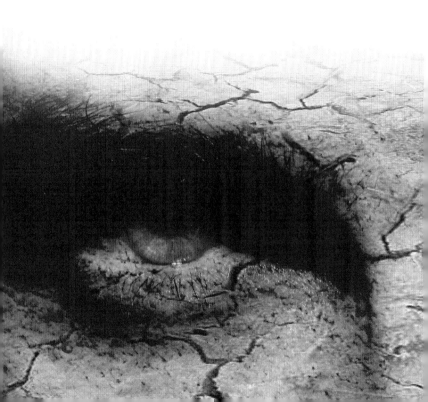

THE ABYSS

The void can go to hell.
The abyss can take a ride.
If you go deep enough into anything
you will come out the other side.

Only wimps resist the dark,
only the ignorant turn from pain.
Only those who get broken down,
are put back together sane.

It's like writing poetry to the ground,
to break your own fall.
When actually you are walking,
not falling at all.

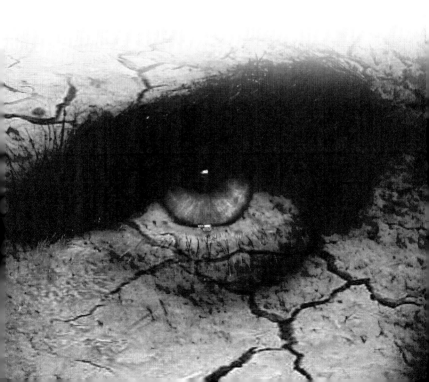

THE CONFESSIONS OF PERSEPHONE

They say I was abducted.
They say that he stole me away.
Kept me captive in the darkness,
to rape and violate.
They say I was helpless, ripe to betray.
I am the golden-haired maiden Kore after all.
But they were wrong.

The truth is that I became bored with Olympus.
The Gods of the living and all their bickering.
I was young and impetuous.
I followed my heart.
It led me astray.
If you don't believe me ask Hecate.
My one faithful witness.
She is not the patron saint of witches for nothing.

It was a long time ago now.
But I remember the small white flower in the field far
away from my mother.
The fragrance of Narcissus.
The sweet allure.
The promise of sin and what I might discover.

And then he came for me.
Riding a chariot pulled by black horses.
I was not afraid.
I knew he was my kin.

He who lives with the souls of the damned.
Knows only the dead for company.
The only one who knows how to touch me.
The hidden brother of my father.
Oh and when the earth closed over us.
There was magic.

No mystery was hidden.
No shadows forbidden.
I would have stayed forever.
But my dear mother Demeter pronounced it tragic.
She laid her mantle of misery upon the earth.
So that nothing could grow, no seeds would sow.
How could she understand the beauty of darkness.
Until she knew how to grieve?

They say that if you eat the fruit of the underworld you
will never leave.
I was very careful to mind my fate.

They say I ate six seeds from the pomegranate.
But actually it was seven.
Three for the earth.
Three for hell.
One for heaven.

I am not the reluctant Queen of the Underworld.
I am the one who mediates.
The weaver of dark and light.
The one who illuminates.
The one who frees.
The daughter of the mother
who needed to discover.
The one who initiates.

Only the Queen of Heaven,
would take Hades as her lover.

Part Two

Falling in the River of Grace

THE YONI VERSE BURLESQUE

I used to say that the Yoniverse,
was in the middle of her greatest ever striptease,
and that I have a front row seat.

But I was wrong.

Actually it's a Burlesque show.
And it's not a seat,
it's the eye of a hurricane.
And to the tune of 'Black Betty'
she is peeling off garments,
so quickly now.
I am mesmerized.

Her veils fall over my eyes,
at first blinding
then clearing my vision.
Throwing swords,
which never fail to hit target.

Although they are not swords,
but boomerangs.

She will never reveal everything.

And right now,
I am so gripped,
by what her next move might be.
That I cannot breathe.

Only gasp at the perplexing perfection of her.

Surrender completely.
And laugh and cry at the same time.

FALLING

I was sitting beside the river of Grace.

Marveling at how vast and wide she is.
When you came along and knelt beside me,
and I fell right in.

How can I sing her song loud enough?

"Listen,"
She sings through me.

Grace comes when you completely accept
and deepen into the life you have exactly as it is.
Without trying to make it different.

The bridges we have burned, were not ones
she could have crossed anyway.

What is left of us.
What does not fit Grace.
Will now be shed.
As easily as these skins have fallen.

As together, we float in bliss.

In the space
between the
out-breath
and the in.

You and me.
The mayor of Armageddon's wife.

Free.
In the silent abyss.

Falling.
Towards life.

EMBODYING LOVE

I said to Love.

"Why did you keep me in the waiting room for so long,
without even anything decent to read before calling me in?"

Love laughed and handed me the book of creation myths.

But the thing is
I have no time to read them
now that

I am so busy
embodying them.

MID LIFE CRISIS

In the middle of your life you stop.
You are either at the point of knowing
what it is you truly want.
Or you have forgotten.

Immobilised and anxious, you stop the climb.
You are waiting for a sign from heaven.

It comes in the form of the master.
Appearing in his most powerful regalia.
Low to the ground and soft spoken, heart broken.
Open.
The king of everything.

His sovereignty extends far beyond the lands you know.
He tells you to prepare for a decisive move.
He tells you that you are the first child of thunder.
He touches you and you wonder,
how nobody ever noticed you are the ocean.

You are the manifester.
The gatherer of resources.
Your libation cup of devotion,
is deep and never empty.

You are correcting, shaking, rousing things.
You startle what is far, bring fear to what is near.
You must go out to the ancestral temple.
Make sacrifice on the earth altar.
Offer up your exile and your fear.

You are the priestess in the ceremony of your life.
The bringer of fertility.
The love maker.
The initiator.

You are the one who reads the signs in dreaming.
Divines the meaning,
and awakens.

Look at what you do not want to see.
Make preparations.
Be sincere, honest and true.
Most of all to you.

When everything comes into view,
you will know what to do.
You will fall.
And the falling will lift you.
And carry you through.

COMPASSION

Somebody once said,
"Start working for God, but keep quiet about it."

Well this is the Kali Yuga.
Try working for the Goddess
and keeping it even remotely quiet.

I mean she inhales oil slicks exhales flowers.
She keeps new galaxies in her pockets,
as loose change to give away to the needy,
for goodness sake.

A SOLSTICE BLESSING

If it feels like the shortest day,
is snapping at your heels.
And there is a hole somewhere through,
which your joy is leaking.
Stop.
And let the darkness receive you.
As you would surrender to a lover.
If your arduous attentiveness,
to the emotional weather.
The shifting sands of other people.
And your ambitions.
Has made your batteries almost flat.
Simply shift your gaze.
If you are exhausted with needing.
Try giving.
If you are cold at night, check.
Did you let the flame keeper fall asleep?
If you really must think of something.
Let it be the small birds.
Speak only kind words.
Be grateful.
Take self-compassion to a whole new level.
Cover your self with kisses and affection.
Stay in bed.
Wear Red.
You will never get free by getting even.
So take all of those grudges that are diminishing
your hearts light.
Bring them closer to the flame.
Let them burn.
You have no more business left with fear.
That gift you were expecting.
Is here.
What are you waiting for?
Unwrap it.
I love you.

Dear God,

Thank you for inviting me
to your great celebration of existence.
I had been quietly longing
and working on myself
so that you would show me where
you were having these private parties.
So imagine my delight, to find myself
graciously included.
Yes, I would love to come, in fact I can't wait!
What should I wear?
I noticed that somehow you have neglected to
mention the exact location and the date.
Perhaps I am missing something obvious?
Please let me know, and do it
in a way that is unmistakable.
(Sometimes I make things too complicated.)
Until then, I will keep my diary
pretty much clear,
wear my best dress,
and wait patiently to hear.

Gratefully yours,
Aisha xxx

AURORA BOREALIS OF THE SOUL

Once you have swum.
In the love that does not know how not to love.

Once you are the song.
That does not dwell in right and wrong.
That does not run from evil.

Once you have become that one simple yes.
That will echo and bless you for a thousand lifetimes.

Then you must return to the world.

We imagine awakening of the spirit.
To be like an aurora borealis of the soul.
A spectacular light show for consciousness.
But you know.

It is way more devastating than that.
Because it happens in your heart.

And all you are.
Is in the depth,
of the claw marks you make as you are taken.

From the farthest star.
Back into your body.

But, it's okay.

You have become the arms of Love.

IN THE LION'S MAW

Why I love poetry so much.
Is that you never know where a good one is taking you.
Until it's too late.
And you're prostrated on the ground beneath its paws.
Defenceless.
Stripped.
Freed from superficiality.
Your cup of desire,
thirstily sipped by ravenous lips.

Poetry is fierce.

Because truth needs a sharp tooth.
To bite into the space between your heart and mine.

BOUDICCA AND BEYOND

Once was a spiritual warrior.

I could feel no love.
Only danger.

They called me a heroine.
I felt like a stranger.

I can not remember what
we were fighting about.

Was it something to do with
the dark and the light?

Did we hit the mark?
Or did we sin in the fight?

Can anybody tell me
if the war was won?

And what was done
with the prize?

THE PATH OF THE HEART

We are on a path.
In the way that the blood could say it's on a path,
as it leaves the aorta.
We have been in this cycle
since the sino-atrial node.
The creator who gave us the Pacemaker,
lay down the hidden code.
Within our body.
What you think is a pulse,
is really a wave.
Between your spirit and your soul.
The diastole is equal to the systole.
And the blood and the breath,
from birth until death,
will do its best to flow
in the right direction.

That is why I do not believe in salvation.
Instead, I thank you God for my semi-lunar valves.

And for reminding me I am just as free
as the day that you made me.
But wilder.

FROM HUMILITY TO DIVINITY

Please don't harden.

The most profound protection,
is to be so transparent,
that what you fear,
can pass right through you.

And if you should stumble.
On the rocky road on which we're walking.
Be thankful to have been humbled.

You are closer
both to God,
and to the ground.

A MEDITATION

So, you're standing at a crossroads.
You see three possible directions.

One is the way you have already traveled.
Another is illuminated by a golden glow,
and you can see very far.
The third is obscured by a thick deep haar.

So, you return to your foundational question,
the one you have been asking all your lives.
The one that resides in the dark part of your heart.

When I was a snake.
Which road did I take?
Where did I leave my breath?
What is the freedom that outlives death?
Who am I?

FREEDOM

You seek enduring freedom.
The freedom you will take with you when you die.
The freedom gained by philosophy,
climbing mountains,
running towards the horizon,
orgasm,
is temporal and not yet stable.

The realisation that there are no constraints,
except those which are self imposed.
May be the treasure found in the pit of poverty
or the desert of hopelessness.

Repeatedly enter the abyss.
If you are not bound by seeking pleasure,
or chained to bliss.
You will unhook the bondage to suffering.

You will become anchored in what is.
Which is truly stable.

When you see that you have always been free.
That it cannot be taken from you.

When your freedom is truly stable.
Transformed from an idea,
into something you know.

You are able to truly give yourself to this life.
Because there is nowhere else to go.

A MOON-DROP

There is strength in the things
that can't possibly exist but do.
That might never have happened but did.
And continue to.
I
Myself
Am as strong as a moon-drop.
I find strength in everything.
Which feels.
And is open.
And is true.

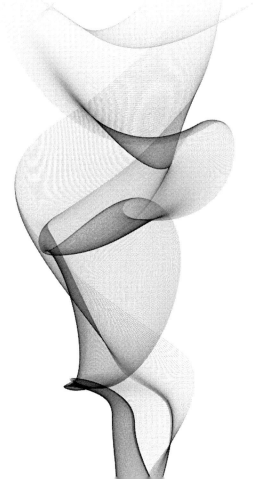

GRACE

Those at the edge,
talk about the edge.

The mystery that lies beyond,
is difficult to speak of.

You need it more
than you have ever needed anything.

This holy place
with no fixed geography.

Whoever you are,
if you talk to me about feeling lonely,
and afraid,
and tired of life.

The promise of my friendship is this.

I will entice you to lean over and peek
a little bit further than you dare to.
And while your eyes are busy adjusting
to the unexpected sight.

I will push you right over.
I am not even kidding.

This is Love talking.

Part Three

The Entire Sky

FISHING

Do not go fishing for love,
draw in your nets.
Walk away from the pier,
and snap your rod into pieces.
Did you think you would be left to starve?

Look,
there is coral below the surface,
and the seeds of pomegranates.
Your Queendom lies waiting for you.

You are closer to the ocean,
than to land now.
Her salty foam,
blended with your tears,
has cleansed the matter from your lashes.
You can see now.

Do not go fishing for love.
Draw in your nets.
Walk away from the pier.
You thought you had transcended desire.
It is time to stop this thinking.
Your desire is how your soul creates your destiny.
Walk over to the dunes,
and leave your clothing there.

Listen,
your only suffering is
when you fear you may starve.
So you build a boat and go fishing.
Now your craft is torn open.
Allow it to sink.
Did you think you would drown
in the depths of your yearning?

Fall towards the centre of your longing.
Enter your Queendom.
The love that lives there,
is more than enough to go around.

HYMN TO THE BELOVED – PART 1

I try to sense your immanent approach.
It keeps me awake at night.
As though small beetles are crawling through my bones.
I cannot sleep any longer.

If the evening breeze carries a hint
of your incense to my door.
Everything stops.
Nothing else matters but your breadth to my depth.

If you arrive at my gate, naked and panting.
Having flown thousand mile skies between us.
I will swell to draw you into my mystery.
I will devour the miles to smell you.

With you there is no cage, no jailor
and fear cannot breathe.
There is scarce foothold for jealousy.
My every cell you flower and
a grain of sand of a lie is a boulder between us.

I do not know when we will meet.
Perhaps it is approaching.
But your words echo
as you lay on the forest floor dying.
As my last legs failed all attempts
to escape my own demise.

"There will be life after death.
You will recognise me
because we will no longer
be talking about the light.
We will be dancing in the flames."

I have and always will be faithful to you.
If being faithful means that you are the level
against which all else is measured.

All of this.
And I have yet to even mention love.
Maybe I will leave that to Rumi.

"I came and sat in front of you, as I would at an altar.
Every promise made before,
I broke when I saw you."

THE MYSTICAL MARRIAGE

Astrologers say
Water signs match water signs.
But I always find myself drowning.

Taoists say water needs earth,
like the riverbanks.
But only rivers need banks.

Alchemist speak of the mystical marriage.
The conjunction of fire and water.
The meeting of complementary opposites.

Sun, moon.
Hot, cold.
Dry, wet.
Desert, ocean.

The union of divine spirit and earthly soul.
Transcending duality.

I'm ready.

Give me the sun.
Give me the volcano.
Give me the sacred fire that illuminates all of creation.

Until I rise from the ashes.

HELLO AGAIN

Of course I never left you, my darling.
That was just a dream you were having.
You know me like the back of your own hand.
Look, see me.
I am everywhere around you.
You can trust this.
I am the blue moths of your fears.
I am the one you are breathing,
who breathes you.
I went underground, yes.
It was to hold your hand,
through the labyrinths of illusion.

I took off all my clothing for you,
so you would awaken.
Do you remember the days when we set our intention?
When I gave birth to you into a lotus flower?
When I poured lava from my open palms
and made landscapes?

I am still burning.

And now,
here we are.
Directing intention and attention.
Actually changing and charging
molecular and sub atomic activity.

Wow.
Isn't it wonderful!

WHY APHRODITE IS HOT

Oh for goodness sake humanity.
Let me clear up this insanity.
About what Love is and what it's not.
And why Aphrodite's so smoking Hot.

It really is my sacred duty,
and perhaps my vanity.
To gift you truth and love and beauty.
The only thing I have to confess.
Is that I bring you the pearls,
from the Love Goddess.

On the path of the heart,
do your best to prove heresy.
To the notion Love is free from fear, shame and jealousy.

Whoever is pierced by Eros' arrow,
and expects the path to be straight and narrow.
Will only sin, or miss the mark,
In consigning shadow to the dark.

Your suffering is a drama of your deepest core pain.
You will be taken there as you utter my name.

Rather than launching a defensive attack,
deepen down to the source of your lack.
This is the treasure for which you sought.
Not where love is, but where love is not.

Jealousy can be an obsession compulsion,
or a gateway to see what's behind that revulsion.
Don't forget that God draws near,
when you get into bed with your deepest fear.

The heart is a fire purifying as it burns.
Emotional tsunami's just take turns.
But it only hurts when refusing to feel.
The heart that won't hurt is the one that won't heal.

Love will set you free.
Her ways are hot and wet and wild.
After she is -
Aphrodite's child.

But if you only want to know about bliss.
Wait patiently for Pan and Artemis.

SWEET TALK

Some admire your beauty,
but do not be tricked.
You will know how a rose feels
before being picked.

Some compliment the look
of your lovely complexion.
But you may well end up
in their butterfly collection.

Some praise love and truth
and talk about integrity.
But would walk past Jesus
if his dress wasn't pretty.

Some sweet talk
will give you a bellyache.
But words of love that nurture you.
Are impossible to fake.

DAFFODILS

For years I gave my mother daffodils.
For mother's day and birthdays.

Then, one day I gave her lilies.

She said "Oh my favourite flowers!"
I said "I thought that was daffodils?"
She said "No daughter, that's yours."

Women.
We are one body of water.
But we're not the same.

We can enjoy our differences as much as our alikeness.

There is absolutely no famine on self-compassion.
Lets put envy and jealousy to rest.

This is a small gesture of worship.
An appreciation of your splendid emergence.

From me.
To you.

LUNARIA REDIVIVA

Honesty,
is a perennial plant best known
for its seed cases
rather than its flowers.

Each case is
flat, translucent, round and papery.

With successful pollination,

every flower will make a separate moon,

and there are several orbiting each stem.

Completely
vulnerable
transparency
is what
intimacy
looks like

between the yang and the yin.

Now that the walls of separation
are paper thin.

What it feels like
is
not having any skin.

The lunar revival is here.

KINDNESS

The lotus
blossomed in
the fall.

The cherry
blossoms in
the spring.

Still she offers new buds.

Her heart, a pure pink lavish
drawing you deeper into
the fragrance of kindness.

Her audacious bloom.
Softer now.

You will never know if it's safe to give everything.
But it hurts too much not to.

The only thing you get from loving,
is loving.

DESIRE

My gaze is turned directly towards the urn of fire.
The grail is in my left hand.
Spilling over with renewal.

Fully absorbed in desire.
Total surrender.
Fear of dying is an old flame.

This life.
Just as I think I have reached the absolute limit.
My heart broken open as much as it can.
It reveals more.
I don't have a head for heights.
But I am not thinking of safety.

Love is the practitioner.
And we are the practice.

Take me to Ekstasis.
I have no more questions.

FROM ARTEMIS TO PAN

Love me forward.
To intimacy with divinity.

Because Illusion breaks my heart.

I wanted you to want me.
Until I didn't know where you ended and I began.

You said,

"In my fathers house, there are many mansions.
As with your mother's house.
They are all on fire.
Just wait, and carry water.
I will meet you in the clearing."

And I did.

I came to you.
The strength of our magnet was an unstoppable force
drawing us closer until of course.

Arousal.
Awakened from sleep.

And while absence makes the heart grow fonder.
I do wonder.
What it would be like.

Would it be such a disaster?
Artemis and Pan happy ever after?

But this heart we share is perennial.
Not seasonal like a rose.

It only grows in the wildness of these waters
In which we swim.

Where love dives deeper,
or drowns in sadness.

The well of Love will ever quench.
While we are drenched with longing for more.

Once before.
I invited you to walk within my heart if only you'd dare.
But it turned out you already lived there.

Softly again, today.
I love you to eternity.

Whatever will be will be.
While we wait for destiny to out run fate.
I remember what you said to me,
"We are the meeting place between the earth's core and
the farthest star."

How right you are.

I don't know who fired the first arrow.
But I hunt for this romance.

My King.
My Horned God.
My lord of the dance.

HAIKU

Japanese incense burns
He speaks what is true,
heaven listens.
He points his finger,
the entire sky closes.
Nothing in my arms but roses.
I write Haiku.
It rains today in Malibu.

TEMPLE WITHOUT WALLS

I wanted to come home.
So you tore my house down.

I wanted to know what freedom was.
So you brought me burning sage, oil of amber,
the taste of ocean to my lips.

You made my hunger stronger than my comfortable cage.

I wanted the veils to rip.
So you positioned me where I could learn to see,
the wood for the trees.

This home I now inhabit has no ceiling,
and doors that don't quite fit.
Windows that can't be covered,
and a ground I struggle sometimes to stand in,
with joists that bear more than I can.

I wanted to live,
so I died for you.
Only then did you take me as your lover.

And I began to discover.
The difference between destiny and fate.

My God, please watch as I decorate.
This temple, without walls.

INTIMACY

the desert of broken glass
we crawl through
on hands and knees
to reach

that oasis of peace

where the love that we seek
and the love that we meet

care enough
to
work it out.

THE WOMAN AND THE MOON

There was once a woman who looked so long and so
intently at the moon,
that it possessed her and she became the ocean.
She cast off her worldly clothes,
and stripped clean to her soul skin.

She became a seal, a dolphin, a manatee, a selkie.
And although this woman had a lover,
a lover who loved to love her.
He was always so busy looking
forwards and backwards.

That he could not see the hexagons in her eyes
had turned from fire to ice,
that beads of moonlight were forming
dew drops on her lips.

That she had become a siren.

And so she was busy dancing with the waves.
Until one day the woman tired of singing
her heart out to the breeze.
She called up a storm.
And the West Wind answered.
And they became lovers.
And although their dance cannot be spoken of here.
The wind breathed the life back into her soul,
and the woman became happy again.
And even in a state of grace.

But the Western Wind is a wayward, restless wind,
and the Lover, belongs to Love,
and the ocean,
she has her tides,
and the woman,
she is just blown away.

You may think that this is a cautionary tale,
But it is vuja de;
The feeling of something that
has never happened before,
something fresh and new.

A love from which new worlds can be made.

A LOVE POEM

The moon possessed me.
It was high tide.
I was ferocious and savage.
Nowhere to run to, rest or hide.
Profound in feeling, depth and emotion.
Terrified you would leave me
for the calm shores of the ocean.

But you stayed.